St. Francis of Assisi

SAINTS
YOU SHOULD KNOW SERIES

St. Francis of Assisi

Margaret and
Matthew Bunson

Our Sunday Visitor Publishing Division
Our Sunday Visitor, Inc.
Huntington, Indiana 46750

ISBN: 0-87973-783-2 (hardcover)
ISBN: 0-87973-557-0 (softcover)
LCCCN: 91-68358

PRINTED IN THE UNITED STATES OF AMERICA

Cover and text illustrations by Margaret Bunson

Foreword

In this modern age, when so many "superstars" seek followers and fans, it is difficult to understand ideals and values that are everlasting and genuine. Few young people today realize that they are being short-changed, cheated out of eternal truths by the age in which they live. Such truths are not echoing in concerts nowadays, and celebrities seldom talk about the really important things concerning human life.

To begin with, every human being on earth faces not only the trials and challenges of daily living but eternal judgments as well. At the same time, all human beings, young and old, unknown or famous, can tap into the same spiritual forces that exist far beyond time, wealth, status, and society. A truly whole human being, in fact, cannot exist just for pleasure, delights, hobbies, or the accumulation of material goods.

How do people know that the spiritual life is possible for everyone? The Catholic Church has safeguarded such revelation over the centuries, providing not only the evidence of such truths but personalities who embodied some particular spiritual aspect of existence in their own lifetimes. Such goodness, such spiritual beauty, is instantly recognizable, even today. Each one of us has suddenly discovered goodness in another person. A single act of kindness, forgiveness, generosity, or love reminds us of the fact that there are individuals who live in the spiritual plane; individuals who walk with God and reflect His beauty in the world.

This book, the life of St. Francis of Assisi, and those volumes to follow, clearly depict human beings who overcame problems, righted wrongs, comforted their companions, and mirrored the saving love of Jesus Christ to mankind. Francis and the other saints did not follow some hidden or strange path to God. They were like the rest of us, ordinary people who accomplished extraordinary things because they opened themselves to God and to His grace.

St. Francis and those like him will always be the true "superstars" of human existence. Their love, their courage, and their generous service to others endure through their earthly adventures and beyond. Just knowing them enriches us, gives us hope, and perhaps even the daring to make our own world right again for everyone. These are people that we should know.

We would like to thank Father Virgil Cordano, O.F.M., the pastor of Santa Barbara Mission, for his kindness in aiding our research. We would like to thank as well Pam Bury and Roberta Kimmel of the Goleta Public Library. This book and the ones to follow are dedicated to Alex Towpasz, for his own future.

MARGARET AND MATTHEW BUNSON

At the close of the twelfth century, during the long period called the Middle Ages, a man known today as St. Francis of Assisi was born. He lived in a time when many city-states rose to power. It was also an era of great opulence, which is a fancy word for fine houses, expensive clothes, and a desire for luxury and pleasure. Opulence, however, sometimes leads to unhappiness. When people have too many things — too many outfits, even in the latest styles, too many toys — they discover a certain empty feeling inside. A small voice keeps asking if this is all there is: just the enjoyment of material goods.

Francis of Assisi asked all of these questions more than seven hundred years ago. First he asked himself about the truths of life.

Then he asked the world to think about God, nature, the poor, and about the way human beings treated one another. Just looking at the sun and the moon, at mountains and streams, at birds and flowers, taught Francis that God created everyone and everything on earth. In return, God expected human beings to follow His divine plan, which would lead all people to salvation.

Francis believed that Jesus Christ was the only true model of God's plan, and he imitated Christ by changing his own views and the way in which he lived. He did not become angry or cold. He did not judge other people or claim that he alone knew the way. Francis embraced the beauty of God's world, and in that simple act he turned his opulent world upside down with song, with laughter, and with prayer. This is Francis' own story, the adventure of a soul!

ASSISI SOON AFTER FRANCIS' DEATH

Assisi was an ancient city even in Francis' time, dating back to the Roman and Etruscan periods of history. It was located in the province of Perugia, Italy, in the region called Umbria. The nearby city of Perugia was a rival to Assisi, as the city councils of each supported different candidates in the violent and ongoing political and social disputes.

Situated on the side of Mount Subasio, and rising in tiers of pink and white brick, Assisi was actually built on Roman ruins. The first cathedral of the city was erected on the site of an old temple of the god Apollo, and other institutions covered similar pagan remains. Beautiful as it rose on the heights of the mountain, Assisi was very much a city of the Middle Ages. Rubbish and slops — a word for the contents of bed chamber pots and water basins — ended up in the streets or on the heads of passersby.

The wealthier people of Assisi, naturally, kept to their own area on the higher slopes of Subasio, although once a year their villas were attacked by bands of rioting poor. Anyone who felt cheated by the nobles or by life stormed the wealthy part of town to settle their accounts. A cease-fire was always put into effect on that same night, lasting exactly one year, when the poor laborers and servants ran screaming back up the slopes to demand their rights again.

These riots gave the people exercise and a certain relief for their emotions, but they seldom managed to break the stranglehold of the wealthy in Assisi. The political and social wars rolled on, and the cities struggled to survive yet another year. The Middle Ages were a time in world history when plagues, wars, duels, riots, and revolts were taking place everywhere. This was Francis' world, the setting for his remarkable life.

Francis of Assisi was born either in September 1181 or perhaps early in 1182, the son of a wealthy cloth merchant, Pietro di Bernardone, and his beautiful wife, Pica. Known as Giovanna, she was called Pica because she came from Picardy. Pica probably met Pietro while he was on one of his trading tours and moved to Assisi with him after their marriage.

Pietro was on the road most days, going across much of western Europe in search of sales and new products. He no doubt visited the fairs at Paris, Bruges, and Ghent, where the latest styles in materials were shown newly arrived from Alexandria, Mosul, and other exotic ports.

Pietro was away when Francis was born, despite the pleas of his family and friends to stay with Pica as her time for delivery neared. Arriving home after the child was born, Pietro was horrified to hear that his son had been baptized Giovanni. He named him Francisco instead, which meant "Frenchman." Such a name was rather odd, but Pietro insisted on it. The child became Francesco or Francis to one and all.

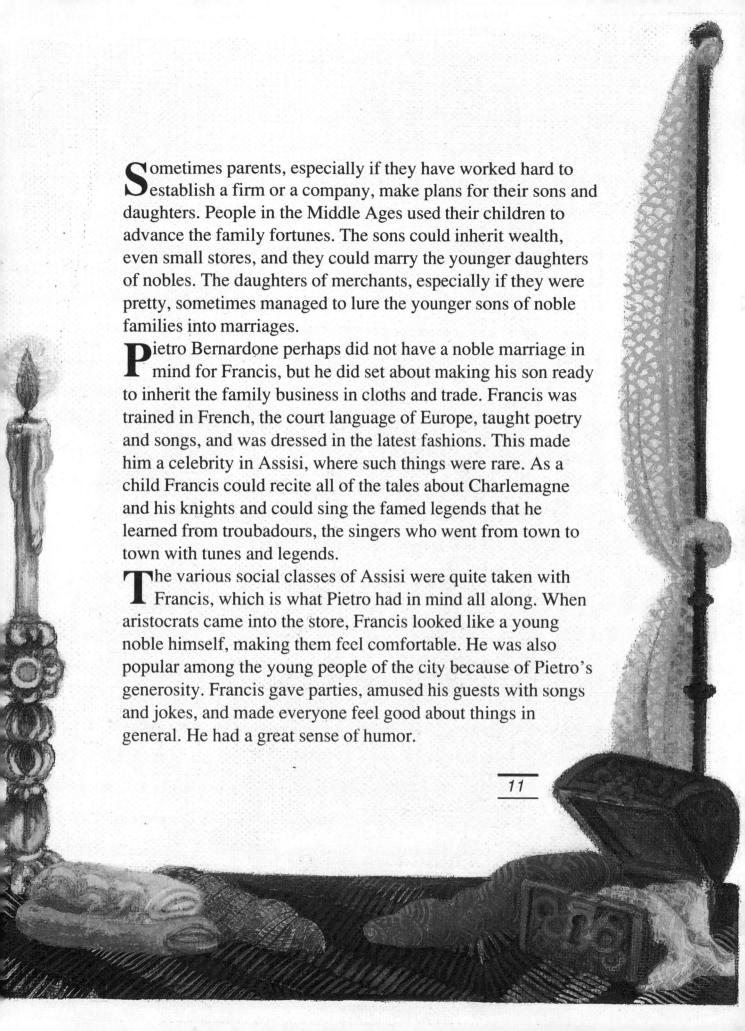

Sometimes parents, especially if they have worked hard to establish a firm or a company, make plans for their sons and daughters. People in the Middle Ages used their children to advance the family fortunes. The sons could inherit wealth, even small stores, and they could marry the younger daughters of nobles. The daughters of merchants, especially if they were pretty, sometimes managed to lure the younger sons of noble families into marriages.

Pietro Bernardone perhaps did not have a noble marriage in mind for Francis, but he did set about making his son ready to inherit the family business in cloths and trade. Francis was trained in French, the court language of Europe, taught poetry and songs, and was dressed in the latest fashions. This made him a celebrity in Assisi, where such things were rare. As a child Francis could recite all of the tales about Charlemagne and his knights and could sing the famed legends that he learned from troubadours, the singers who went from town to town with tunes and legends.

The various social classes of Assisi were quite taken with Francis, which is what Pietro had in mind all along. When aristocrats came into the store, Francis looked like a young noble himself, making them feel comfortable. He was also popular among the young people of the city because of Pietro's generosity. Francis gave parties, amused his guests with songs and jokes, and made everyone feel good about things in general. He had a great sense of humor.

A MIDDLE AGES MARKETPLACE

The rage at the time in Italy was a dance performed by groups of young people in the streets or in the courts of the larger homes. These dancers called themselves the *tripudianti*, which meant "the stompers." Francis led the way in "stomping" through the streets until the Church officials halted the dances. On the feast day of St. Ercolano, the patron of the "stompers," all of the young people sang and danced in his honor. In the lead was Francis, throwing coins to the poor and singing his songs.

He did not shine in the classroom, however. Perhaps the local teachers did not inspire him. The town of Assisi was rather dull and plain when compared to the cities that Francis visited with his father. Pietro continued to take Francis to the fairs across Europe and especially to France, where the young man perfected his French accent. He also learned enough about the mannerisms and styles of the nobles to pass for one. This was part of Pietro's plans for his son and heir.

13

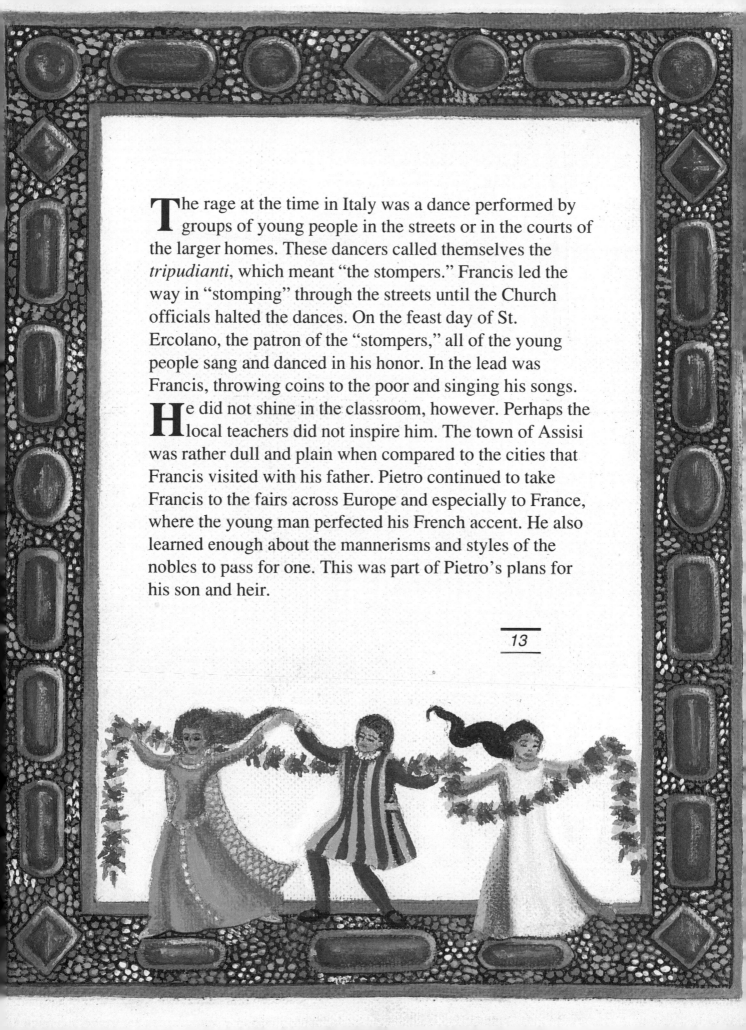

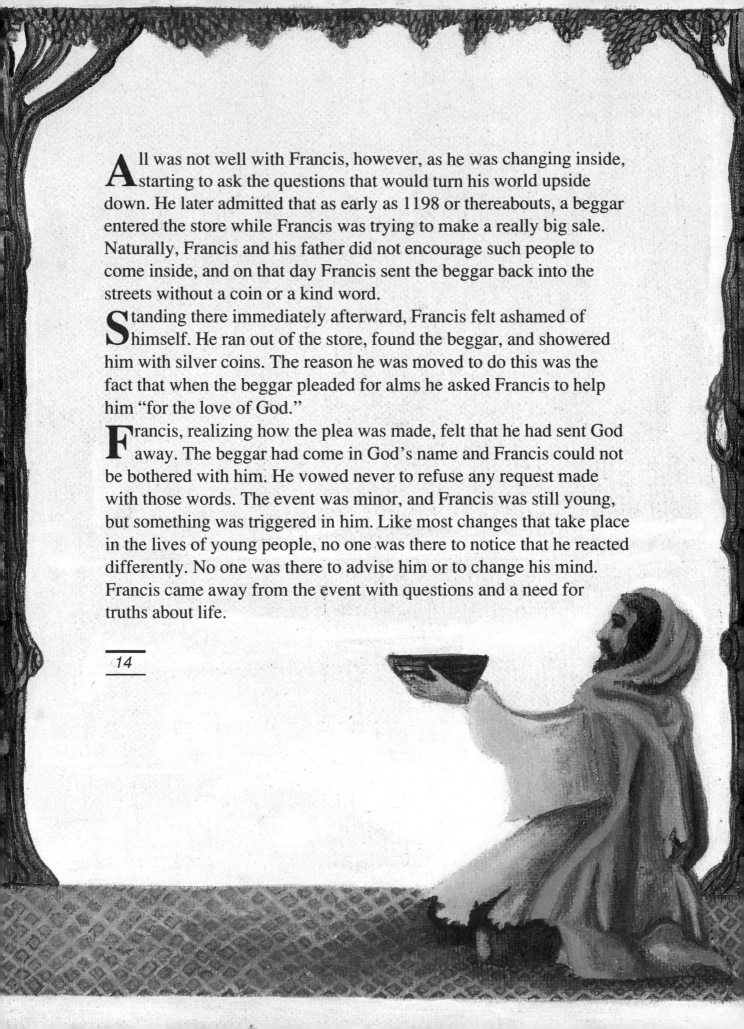

All was not well with Francis, however, as he was changing inside, starting to ask the questions that would turn his world upside down. He later admitted that as early as 1198 or thereabouts, a beggar entered the store while Francis was trying to make a really big sale. Naturally, Francis and his father did not encourage such people to come inside, and on that day Francis sent the beggar back into the streets without a coin or a kind word.

Standing there immediately afterward, Francis felt ashamed of himself. He ran out of the store, found the beggar, and showered him with silver coins. The reason he was moved to do this was the fact that when the beggar pleaded for alms he asked Francis to help him "for the love of God."

Francis, realizing how the plea was made, felt that he had sent God away. The beggar had come in God's name and Francis could not be bothered with him. He vowed never to refuse any request made with those words. The event was minor, and Francis was still young, but something was triggered in him. Like most changes that take place in the lives of young people, no one was there to notice that he reacted differently. No one was there to advise him or to change his mind. Francis came away from the event with questions and a need for truths about life.

Meanwhile, the social and political tides of Europe were beginning to wash over Italy and its cities. Two ruling factions, or political sides, began to quarrel across the land. Assisi was caught up in the struggle, as it supported the dukes of Spoleto, noblemen who backed the cause of the Holy Roman emperors, the powerful rulers who claimed to be the true heirs of the ancient Roman Empire. The people supporting the emperors were called Ghibellines, and they opposed the Guelfs, people who were allies of the Pope. The duke of Spoleto, seeing that the imperial forces were going to lose, placed himself on the side of the Pope. This made the people of Assisi quite furious. They called him a traitor and stormed the nearby castle of Rosca Alta. The building was empty at the time, so it was a vain threat.

Francis was one of the young men chosen to storm the fortress on Mount Subasio, just above Assisi. When the attack was completed, the city declared itself an imperial ally, which brought a rapid response from the Pope. Assisi was condemned publicly. The doors of the churches were closed and sealed by wooden planks, and the statues and sacred vessels were covered with dark cloths. The people of Assisi were upset, naturally, as the papal condemnation brought about terrible results. When people died in the town, there were no burial ceremonies available to them. Their sobbing relatives, unable to place them in their graves without the Church's blessings, had to bring the coffins and pile them up next to the churches, praying for better days.

In 1200, conditions had not changed for the better, and the young men of Assisi were led into a war against nearby Perugia. The two sides actually argued and called each other names for about two years, becoming angrier and more excited. To the blare of trumpets, with the cheers of their fellow townspeople ringing in their ears, a band of knights rode out of Assisi to defend the city's honor. Francis was among them, dressed by a proud Pietro, who gave him a horse and the finest armor that money could buy so that his son could ride with the nobles. The poorer soldiers had to walk to war, with little to defend themselves when the battle began.

Francis was delighted, of course, because the campaign brought to life all of the songs that he had sung about knights and war in the past. He was now a knight, a legendary warrior about whom the minstrels and troubadours sang from town to town. Gallantry, honor, chivalry, and other warrior traditions appeared in his heart as he led his horse to battle.

The campaign turned sour in an instant! The men of Assisi rode for several hours and then met the enemy on the banks of the Tiber River. There many of Francis' friends and neighbors were cut down by the foe. They were hacked by swords, pierced with arrows and lances, and some even drowned. Their horses, wounded, screamed and fell on the young riders, pinning them under the water and snapping their spines. The cavalry charges of the enemy came like giant avalanches, smashing into the colorfully dressed knights who had entered a war without understanding any part of it.

Francis of Assisi was captured by the Perugians and was led away to the dungeons of the city's castle. Only a few of his friends were lucky enough to come out of the battle alive, and they joined him in the dank stone pits.

He was imprisoned for over a year there, gaining a reputation for his response to his destiny. Francis did not complain, and he was noted for trying to improve the moods and conditions of his fellow prisoners.

One man who served there with him said that Francis announced: "I rejoice because one day I shall be venerated as a saint all over the world." His companions thought he was sick with fever, and his physical condition did take a turn for the worse because of his treatment.

Pietro, paying a large sum, finally managed to secure Francis' release, and he returned to Assisi, where the people celebrated peace and the return of the captives.

18

Back home at last, much to the relief of his mother, Pica, Francis took part in the many celebrations being held in town. His old activities did not appeal to him very much, however, and he watched his friends working very hard to have fun. It seemed that everyone tried to sing and dance in a rather mindless way. They repeated the same old jokes, told the same gossip over and over, and they laughed too long and just a little too loud.

He had been through a terrible trial in the prison of Perugia. He was aware of events and people that were far more important than jokes or gossip. Francis was involved as well in the mental process called growing up, and the hard truths about life made everything else seem rather stupid.

He still liked knighthood and chivalry, despite the slaughter on the battlefield, and he joined in the admiration of his friends for a nobleman named Walter of Brienne. This proud, boisterous — which means loud and enthusiastic — warrior was a mercenary knight, a man who fought for money in the battlefields of Italy. There were enough such arenas to keep him busy, as the whole of Europe was troubled at the time. Walter's tales and warrior ways led the young men of Assisi into yet another knightly quest, or search for adventure. They mounted up once again to join him in Spoleto, where glory awaited all who survived the battlefields. Their numbers were certainly fewer, but the young men rode off in search of adventure again.

FRANCIS AS A YOUNG MAN

Pietro, who had been alarmed by Francis' condition when he returned from Perugia, was delighted that his son now planned to be part of the military campaign. He provided him with a magnificent suit of armor and with all of the fancy weapons and symbols that would mark Francis as a young man who was going places. Pietro, naturally, hoped that Francis would bring honor to the family name in the war and would improve the family fortunes by becoming a celebrated warrior.

Pica was quieted with stern words when she tried to tell her husband that their son was ill. Pietro waved good-bye to Francis and his companions, and once again Assisi cheered the small army departing for the battlefield.

Pietro, fortunately, did not witness the rather odd event that took place near the city of Spoleto. There Francis met a knight who was in a sorry state, with dented armor and no sign of rank or distinction. Seeing the knight's rather run-down condition, Francis gave him his expensive cloak. The cloak covered up the dents in the knight's armor and made him look reasonably prosperous. That action had a historical meaning as well. A man named Martin of Tours, another saint, had once given half of his cloak to a beggar who, in a dream that Martin had later on, turned out to be Christ.

21

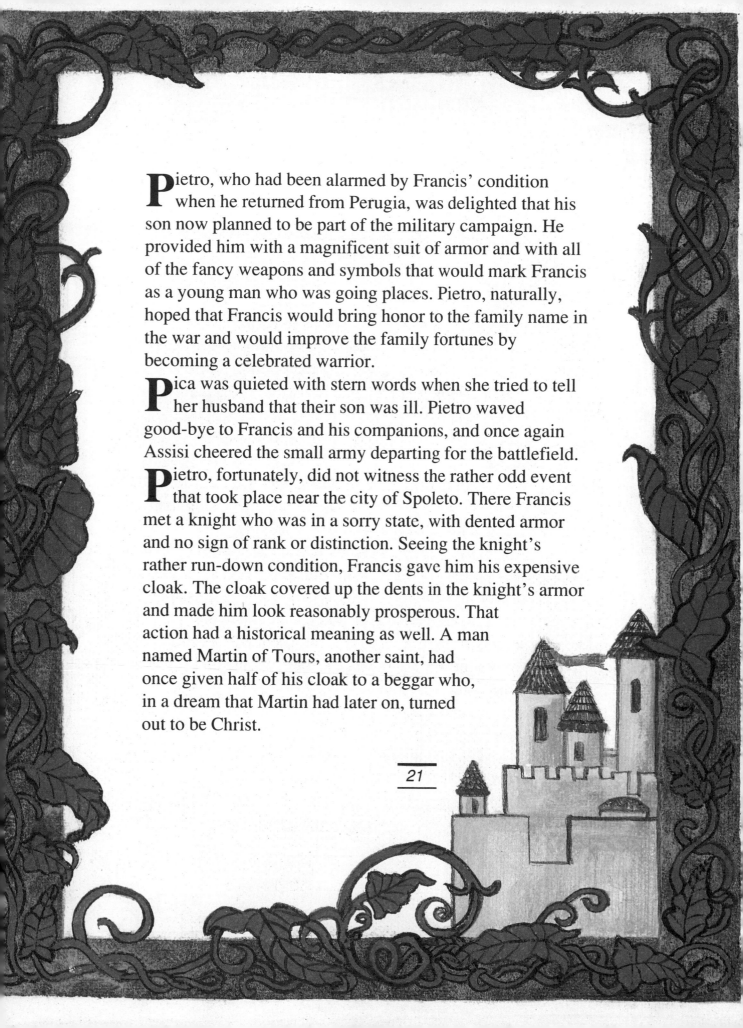

As Pica had sensed, Francis was too ill to continue on the march, and he withdrew from the campaign. Selling his armor, he stayed in Spoleto for a time, returning to Assisi dressed as a peasant. Pietro almost had a fit when he realized that the armor, horse, and fancy clothes had been sold. He had put himself into a financial bind in order to make the money available for his son, and now he had nothing to show for it.

Pietro, along with many of the townspeople, also had some doubts about Francis' courage. Some thought that the young man was a coward who could not face the war. Others said they had always known he was slightly crazy. All they knew was that Francis had gone off to war dressed like a knight champion and then had come home penniless and acting strangely. Not only did Francis dress like a beggar, he also prayed a great deal and gave alms to anyone who asked him. It was enough to make Pietro weep. He yelled at Francis, took out his anger on Pica, and came to the conclusion that someone must have cursed him for an unknown reason.

Poor Pietro, so firmly bound to the world, so tightly tied to his cloth store and his rounds of sales, had no way of knowing that Francis had started a new life. Francis was not a coward, not a maniac, and certainly he was not the result of a curse on Pietro's head. This young man had been chosen by Almighty God to confound his opulent age, which is a fancy way of saying that Francis had been declared the one to set his own world on its ear.

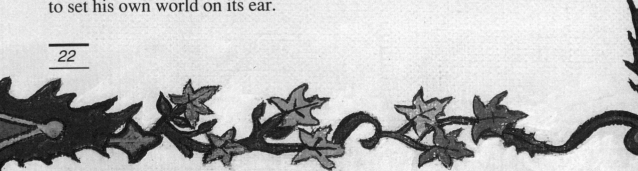

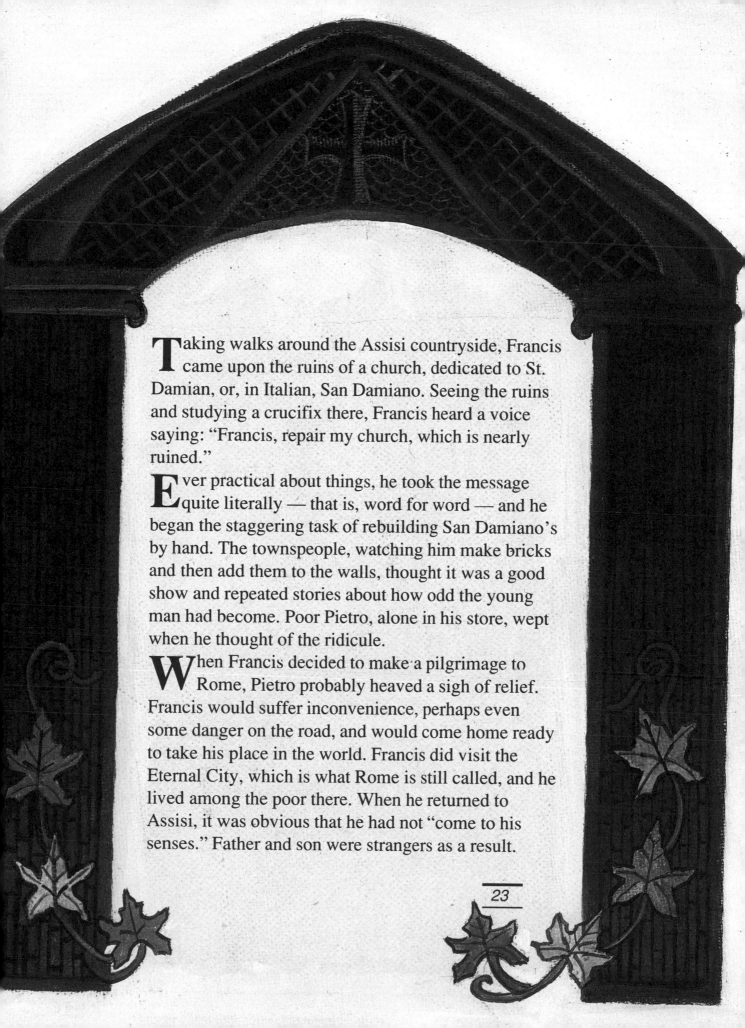

Taking walks around the Assisi countryside, Francis came upon the ruins of a church, dedicated to St. Damian, or, in Italian, San Damiano. Seeing the ruins and studying a crucifix there, Francis heard a voice saying: "Francis, repair my church, which is nearly ruined."

Ever practical about things, he took the message quite literally — that is, word for word — and he began the staggering task of rebuilding San Damiano's by hand. The townspeople, watching him make bricks and then add them to the walls, thought it was a good show and repeated stories about how odd the young man had become. Poor Pietro, alone in his store, wept when he thought of the ridicule.

When Francis decided to make a pilgrimage to Rome, Pietro probably heaved a sigh of relief. Francis would suffer inconvenience, perhaps even some danger on the road, and would come home ready to take his place in the world. Francis did visit the Eternal City, which is what Rome is still called, and he lived among the poor there. When he returned to Assisi, it was obvious that he had not "come to his senses." Father and son were strangers as a result.

23

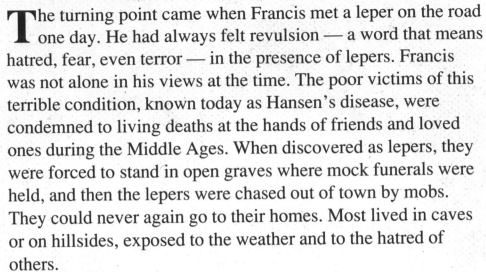

The turning point came when Francis met a leper on the road one day. He had always felt revulsion — a word that means hatred, fear, even terror — in the presence of lepers. Francis was not alone in his views at the time. The poor victims of this terrible condition, known today as Hansen's disease, were condemned to living deaths at the hands of friends and loved ones during the Middle Ages. When discovered as lepers, they were forced to stand in open graves where mock funerals were held, and then the lepers were chased out of town by mobs. They could never again go to their homes. Most lived in caves or on hillsides, exposed to the weather and to the hatred of others.

These victims starved, sat alone with their pain, and faced the slow tormenting end without a single friend. Lepers had to carry bells wherever they went so that people like Francis Bernardone, who felt revulsion at the sight of them, could flee.

Francis, overcoming his own fears and horror, because he knew that it was not pleasing to Christ, gave the leper a kiss of peace, the traditional Christian greeting. He turned away for an instant to celebrate his victory over his own feelings, and when he looked back, the leper was gone. No sight of him remained, and no bell echoed over the hillsides.

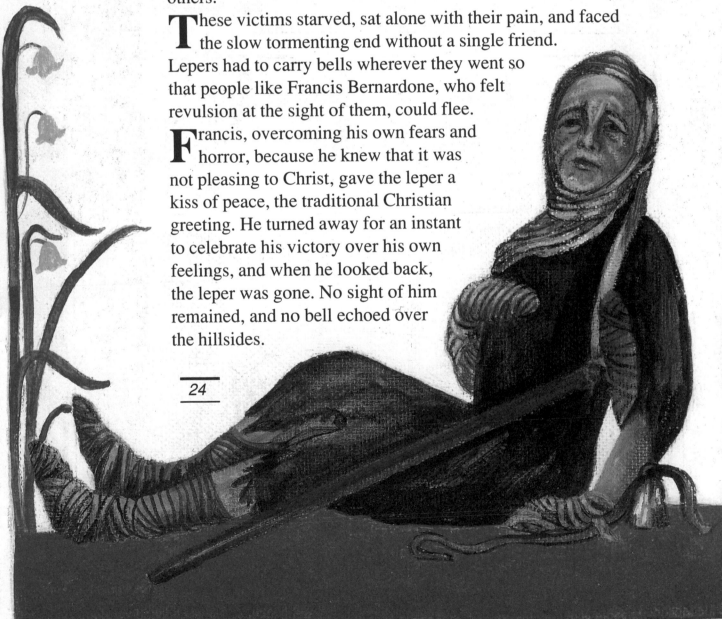

24

Tales of the episode with the leper spread through Assisi, however, and Pietro felt forced into taking drastic steps. He caught Francis and locked him in a closet in their home. The young man was clothed and fed, but he was forbidden to leave the closet by his father.

Pica saw what was happening, and she silently supported Francis, defying Pietro, which took some courage. Whenever Pietro was away she let Francis out of the closet, and they talked and prayed together. As any mother knows her child, Pica sensed that Francis had been chosen by God for a unique and wonderful role in the world.

She was not afraid that he was going to condemn her to a "living death" by caring about a leper. She was also sure that Francis was quite sane about life and the world. Francis was becoming God's instrument on earth, and no human had the right to interfere with that change.

Pietro, of course, was afraid of what the neighbors or officials might say. He was defending what he held to be his most precious object in life: his cloth trade. To him Francis seemed bent on destroying that trade and Pietro's good name.

25

On April 10, 1206, Pietro demanded that his son appear before the city officials to renounce his inheritance. Pietro was placing as much distance between Francis and himself as he could, in order to protect his reputation and his money. When Francis refused to appear before the city court, Pietro went to the bishop of Assisi. Francis came to the bishop's residence humbly and joyfully, knowing that Pietro wanted him legally put aside. He agreed not only to Pietro's demands but astonished everyone by offering even more.

Look, everyone!" Francis announced. "From now on I can say with total freedom, 'My Father who art in heaven.' Pietro Bernardone is no longer my father. I give him back not only his money but all my clothes as well."

Francis then took off everything in front of the people, making the bishop weep and cover him with his own cloak. The prelate — a Latin word used to describe bishops of the Church — understood that Francis had become a true son of Christ. He had no ties with the world, and only the glistening horizons of faith and grace stretched before him.

He was free of the love of money, free of the desire to be "somebody" in the eyes of the world. Francis of Assisi had started on his divinely inspired vocation, or calling. He was going to rebuild the Church, as the voice had asked. It was not just a chapel, however, but all of Christendom, all of Christ's domain on earth.

Francis had asked himself where he was going, and his heart and mind responded easily with the truth. Like every other human being in the world, he was born to make his way through life and then to join his heavenly Father. Life with God does not begin when one dies but when one is born into the world. Life with God is not just a matter of following rules or putting aside temptation. Francis and the thousands of men and women who followed him into the Franciscan Order discovered that loving and serving God made them whole, clean, and unafraid. The world, then as now, demands that humans believe its lies, accept its standards, and repeat its slogans. Only the brave have daring enough to think about eternal values, about death, and about the truth of life itself.

Francis, covered only in the bishop's robe, walked out of Assisi toward San Damiano, but thieves spotted the cloak and knocked him down to steal that too. Francis laughed when he saw what was happening. Still laughing and singing God's praises, he made his way to his first home. There he put on a coarse tunic, working on the church and raising it up as a reborn house of prayer. He had learned about wall fortifications in the years of the wars, when he served Assisi.

Pietro, his father, disappears at this point in history. Did he ever realize that Francis was destined to be world famous, beloved and respected by many faiths? Did he long to embrace him and offer aid? History does not tell us. Pietro had his cloth shop and his money. He seemed to have little else left in his world.

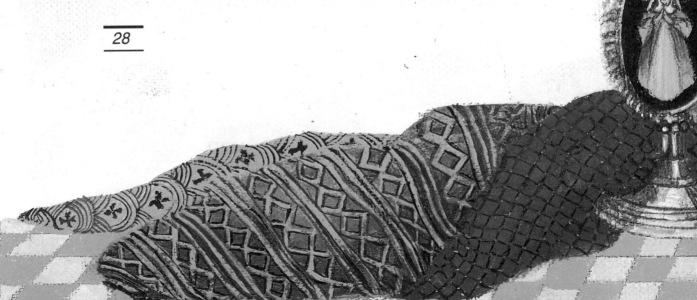

In time Francis moved to a small chapel, called the Portiuncula, where a Benedictine monk celebrated Mass each day. It was during one of these Masses that Francis realized that his real mission was to change the world around him. He was to live as a perfect imitation of Christ, ever loyal and faithful to the Church.

He returned to Assisi as a preacher, but his manner as well as his message was unlike those of other self-styled prophets. Many called for people to kill the priests and to overthrow the Church. Francis, a gifted speaker, talked to the people of Assisi about their personal lives instead. He told them to change their own ways, not to worry about others.

Remembering him as a young man, the people were at first amused by his daring. They reminded him of the fact that they "knew him when." Francis did not complain but continued to speak of loneliness, of pain, of sin, which isolates humans from God. The people listened, stopped laughing, and slowly began to change their own ways of thinking. Some even decided to put aside their careers to follow Francis on his royal road of perfection.

29

The first to follow Francis was a man named Bernard of Quintavalle, an expert in civil and canon law at the University of Bologna, one of the truly wealthy persons in Assisi. Bernard had watched Francis endure the unkind words, mud, even stones, thrown at him by the people of Assisi as he began to call them to perfection. He was touched by Francis' humility and gentle ways, and he invited the young man to dinner. Francis accepted, restricting his meals to simple fare, however, and in time he was visiting Bernard frequently. The people of Assisi, of course, were impressed, and one can only guess what Pietro thought of when he heard that his disinherited son was being so honored.

Bernard listened and learned, and one night he stayed up to spy on his saintly guest, observing how Francis prayed. He later said that Francis rose from his bed and started by saying "God! God!" Francis remained in prayer throughout the night, watched by Bernard, and in the morning's light the great lawyer decided to become one of his followers.

I am resolved in my heart to leave the world and to follow you in whatever you bid me," he told Francis. Bernard was thus the first of thousands of men and women who would lay aside the illusions and the tricks of the world to imitate Christ.

30

Francis, naturally, was a bit surprised by this offer and was not entirely sure that this was what God had in mind. He decided to consult the Gospels, or the "Good News," another name for the Bible. Joined by a third man, a friend of Bernard, named Peter of Catania, Francis set out with Bernard to the nearby church of San Nicolo. After Mass they went to the Gospel, which was on the lectern there. Opening the book three times and reading the verse that appeared each time, the three men were astounded.

The readings were rather to the point: "If you would be perfect, go, sell what you possess and give to the poor, and you will have treasure in heaven; and come, follow me" (Matthew 19:21), "Take nothing for your journey, no staff, nor bag, nor bread, nor money" (Luke 9:3), and "If any man would come after me, let him deny himself and take up his cross daily and follow me" (Luke 9:23).

Francis of Assisi's days as a wandering hermit were over. With Bernard and Peter he had begun a great spiritual adventure that would change the lives of millions in time. The three were soon joined by others, such as Sylvester, Giles, and Angelo Tancredi from Rieti. In time there were Philip the Tall, Sabbatini, and John della Capella. The most famous of the early Franciscans, however, was Brother Juniper, the companion of Francis, whose simplicity and ability to live the ideals of the Franciscans brought Francis to exclaim: "If only I had a whole forest of Junipers!"

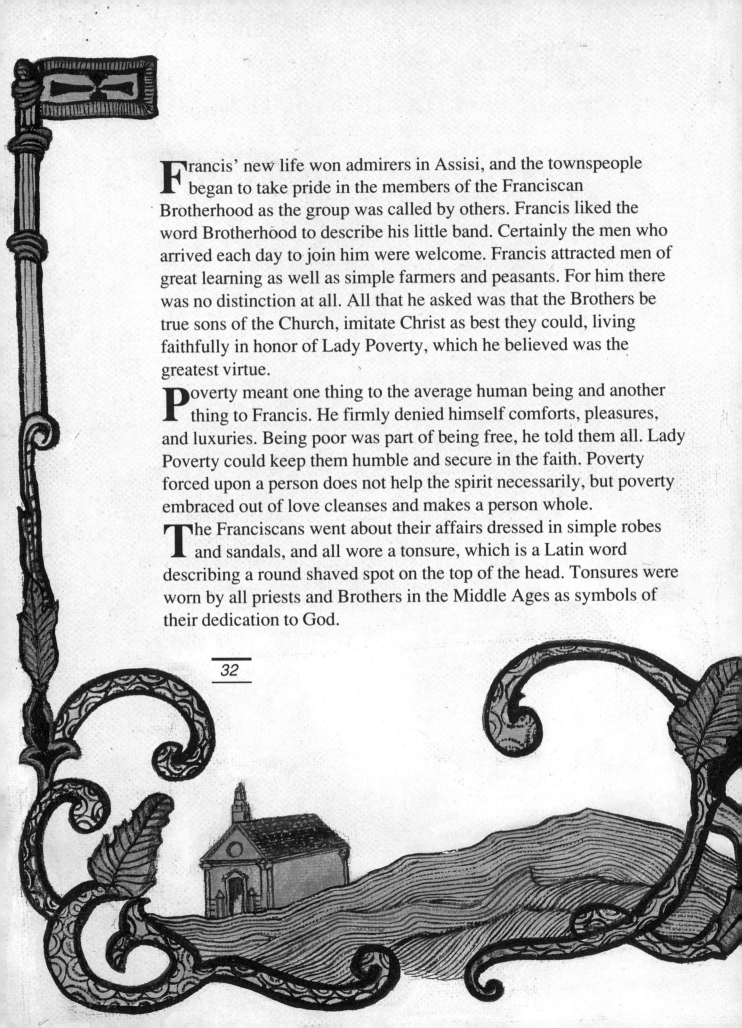

Francis' new life won admirers in Assisi, and the townspeople began to take pride in the members of the Franciscan Brotherhood as the group was called by others. Francis liked the word Brotherhood to describe his little band. Certainly the men who arrived each day to join him were welcome. Francis attracted men of great learning as well as simple farmers and peasants. For him there was no distinction at all. All that he asked was that the Brothers be true sons of the Church, imitate Christ as best they could, living faithfully in honor of Lady Poverty, which he believed was the greatest virtue.

Poverty meant one thing to the average human being and another thing to Francis. He firmly denied himself comforts, pleasures, and luxuries. Being poor was part of being free, he told them all. Lady Poverty could keep them humble and secure in the faith. Poverty forced upon a person does not help the spirit necessarily, but poverty embraced out of love cleanses and makes a person whole.

The Franciscans went about their affairs dressed in simple robes and sandals, and all wore a tonsure, which is a Latin word describing a round shaved spot on the top of the head. Tonsures were worn by all priests and Brothers in the Middle Ages as symbols of their dedication to God.

As people arrived each day, Francis understood that the Brotherhood needed a rule of life. He wrote the *Regula Prima*, the "First Rule," stressing the need for poverty and for austerity. Austerity is a way of life in which the individual avoids pleasures, comforts, and treats — anything that would distract the person from God and service to others. Above all, the Brotherhood was required to be faithful to the Pope and to remain true sons of the Church in all things.

In the spring of 1209, after prayer and discussion, Francis and some of his original companions set out for Rome, walking the highways and byways of Italy with song and with prayer. They expected that the Pope would be happy to receive them.

In Rome, however, at the Lateran Palace, the residence of the Pope at the time, the guards took one look at this group of wandering beggars and threw them out. The Pope himself supposedly glimpsed them, and he wanted nothing to do with such a weird group. Meanwhile, the bishop of Assisi, the one who had draped his own cloak around Francis when Pietro demanded that his son be disinherited, had become an archbishop and was in Rome. He introduced Francis to Cardinal Giovanni, who had great influence in the papal court. There was no need for assistance from Cardinal Giovanni, however, because Pope Innocent III was having a troubled night on account of the little man in the ragged brown robe.

The first night Pope Innocent III dreamed about a palm tree that was sprouting from the earth. When the palm had grown to an enormous size, shading everything, the Pope was told that the tree was Francis of Assisi, the one who had been called a bum and booted out of the palace. Innocent III got up the next morning and asked that the little band of beggars be found. There was no problem in this because Cardinal Giovanni had them all safely in his residence. He brought them before the Pope almost at once.

As the cardinals assembled for the interview, Francis explained his Brotherhood and his dream. Many of the cardinals thought that he meant well but did not understand human nature. They explained that the average human being would soon drop dead trying to live the way Francis did personally. Others pointed to the Gospels and asked if the teachings there were wrong. Pope Innocent III, hearing the debate, told Francis to pray for a few days and then return with new ideas or better explanations.

The Holy Father, however, was not going to enjoy the second night either. He dreamed that he was in the Lateran Basilica — a type of church that dates to the Roman era in design and has a special rank — and that he was wearing his tiara and his robes. The Lateran Basilica was leaning to one side, threatening to crash down on the Pope's head. Then a small man in a ragged brown robe appeared and put one hand to the wall, gently supporting it and forcing it back into place. The Pope did not have to be told who the man was this time. It was Francis of Assisi.

The following morning Pope Innocent III gave Francis his personal approval, in words only, and told him to continue with the Brotherhood, to return at a later time to have approval from Rome for his work.

The Franciscans returned to Assisi with the approval, at least verbally, and the Brotherhood began its work in earnest. Francis chose a site for the first foundation at Rivo Torto, an area near Assisi that had once been part of a hospital for lepers. If any of the Brothers felt revulsion at the thought, they conquered their own weaknesses, as Francis had years before.

They lived in simple thatched huts, made out of daub and wattle, a cementlike substance that dried hard and could be painted white. The roofs were made out of sticks and straw, called thatchwork. The men slept on the ground or on wooden planks, which had their individual names scratched into them. There were no chairs or tables, and the meals were simple. These "simple" meals, in fact, were so small that one night a young Brother groaned that he fully expected to die during the night from starvation. Francis, hearing his complaints, ordered everyone to eat another meal to fill him up and to save him embarrassment. The others were probably quite happy to make the young man feel better.

Francis also started a simple rule that said: "No work, no eat." This brought everyone out to the fields or to the various work sites, because even the starvation diet was better than nothing at all.

36

THE PORTIUNCULA AS IT IS PRESERVED TODAY

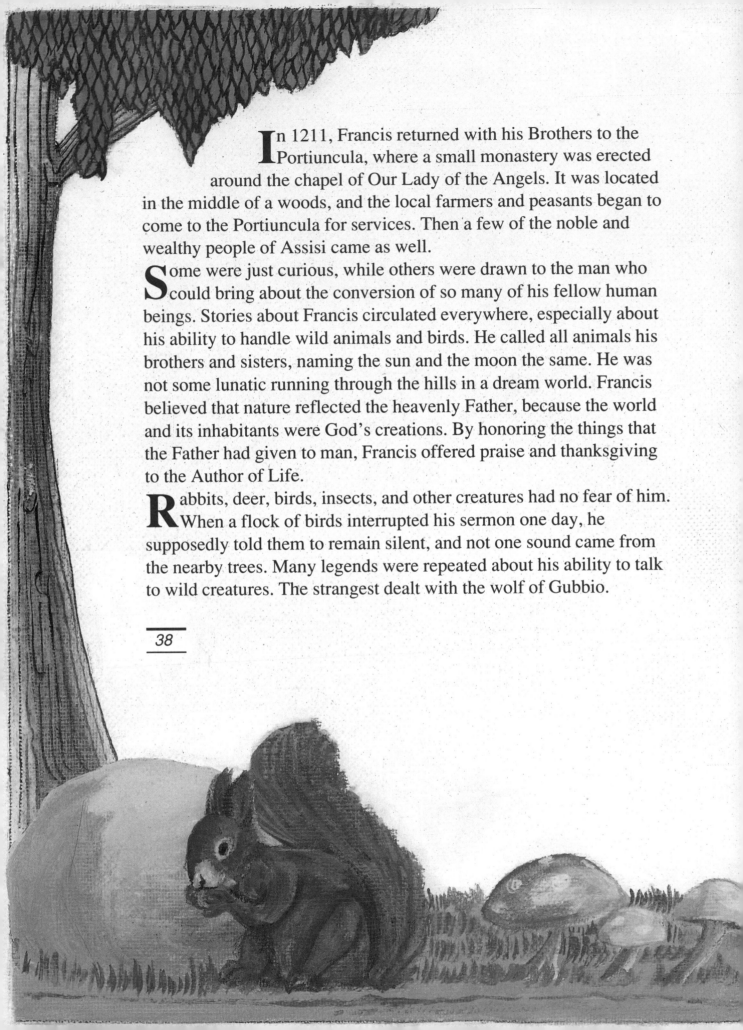

In 1211, Francis returned with his Brothers to the Portiuncula, where a small monastery was erected around the chapel of Our Lady of the Angels. It was located in the middle of a woods, and the local farmers and peasants began to come to the Portiuncula for services. Then a few of the noble and wealthy people of Assisi came as well.

Some were just curious, while others were drawn to the man who could bring about the conversion of so many of his fellow human beings. Stories about Francis circulated everywhere, especially about his ability to handle wild animals and birds. He called all animals his brothers and sisters, naming the sun and the moon the same. He was not some lunatic running through the hills in a dream world. Francis believed that nature reflected the heavenly Father, because the world and its inhabitants were God's creations. By honoring the things that the Father had given to man, Francis offered praise and thanksgiving to the Author of Life.

Rabbits, deer, birds, insects, and other creatures had no fear of him. When a flock of birds interrupted his sermon one day, he supposedly told them to remain silent, and not one sound came from the nearby trees. Many legends were repeated about his ability to talk to wild creatures. The strangest dealt with the wolf of Gubbio.

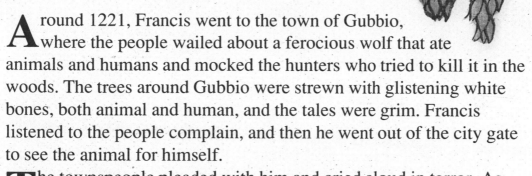

Around 1221, Francis went to the town of Gubbio, where the people wailed about a ferocious wolf that ate animals and humans and mocked the hunters who tried to kill it in the woods. The trees around Gubbio were strewn with glistening white bones, both animal and human, and the tales were grim. Francis listened to the people complain, and then he went out of the city gate to see the animal for himself.

The townspeople pleaded with him and cried aloud in terror. As Francis neared the woods, in fact, they could hear the howl of the beast encircling the town. Deep within the forest the wolf approached Francis, who made the sign of the cross, saying: "Brother Wolf, come here! You will not eat Brother Ass [Francis' own nickname for himself and his body] and I command you not to harm anyone else." The wolf listened and eyed Francis with cunning.

39

Francis then told the animal that he wished to make peace between it and the people of Gubbio. The wolf followed Francis back to the town, where the people almost fainted at the sight of it. Francis then sternly announced to the citizens there that they were not the most exciting or kindest human beings that he had ever met in his life. They were like human wolves, in fact, attacking the poor and the defenseless, making fun of the sick and the old. The people listened, with one eye on the wolf, and in time agreed to provide the animal fresh food each day. In return the wolf had to protect Gubbio and its residents. This arrangement worked well for two years, when the wolf died of old age. The people buried the creature in their chapel, as they were proud of its devotion. Over the next years, people from other towns made fun of the tale. No matter how many times the people of Gubbio insisted that the story was true, people laughed and doubted them. They stopped laughing in 1873, when excavations — the digging activities that are used around the world to uncover ruins or buried sites — were started in Gubbio's chapel. The remains of the wolf of Gubbio were unearthed, protected by a loving townspeople who remembered Francis of Assisi.

40

As Francis was attracting men from around Europe, he also had influence on the people of Assisi. Many of his friends from the past remembered him and wondered at the changes that had taken place in his life. One of these was a young woman named Clare Offreduccio, who belonged to a very wealthy family in the town. Clare heard tales about Francis, probably talking with him personally in the early days.

At first wild tales ran through Assisi about how mad Francis had become. The story about Pietro disinheriting him would have spread like wildfire through the town. In time, of course, the people recognized that God had chosen Francis for a special task. Then they all claimed that they knew it from the start. They probably boasted that Francis had confided in them personally, asking their help and receiving it. People do that sometimes. They have to pretend that they understood all along.

While Francis was visiting the Pope and causing his strange dreams, Clare was becoming a very special human being in her own right. She knew that her family planned to marry her to some wealthy young man so that the fortunes of both clans could be joined. She had other plans, however, and she practiced the same sort of lifestyle that Francis did, only she had to keep her ways secret. Clare gave alms to the poor, visited the sick, and lived as simply as possible, giving many hours to prayer.

The opulent life that her family had in Assisi seemed rather pointless to Clare, especially when she saw the suffering all around them. In the Middle Ages, as in some areas of the modern world, people were either rich or poor. The wealthy had servants, fine houses, beautiful clothes, and protection. The poor had illness, pain, cold, and the cruelty of their masters who wanted to gain from their labors without giving anything in return.

ST. CLARE

Clare heard Francis preaching one day, and his words gave her courage to do what she knew God wanted for her life. On Palm Sunday, 1212, the bishop of Assisi, who knew what was in her heart, noticed that Clare had forgotten to take a blessed palm from the altar. He marched down the aisle of the church to give her one personally. In this way he was telling her that he approved of her decision and would help her.

Clare went to Francis, who cut off her beautiful hair and then clothed her in a simple brown robe and a veil. She went to live with some Benedictine nuns so that she would be safe and could learn about the religious life. Her father, naturally, was having the same sort of worries and concerns suffered by Pietro years before. Clare, however, stood as firm as Francis, and in time she was able to make her final vows.

In 1215, she became the head of a small group of Franciscan women in a little house erected for her beside San Damiano Church. In time her mother and two sisters joined her there, as did many other women, including members of the famous Florentine family called the Ubaldini. The sight of wealthy, noble women taking up the lifestyle of Francis of Assisi caused quite a stir throughout Europe.

Clare and her companions formed the Second Order of the Franciscans, called the Poor Clares. She died in 1253 and was canonized — the process by which the Church declares certain individuals worthy of sainthood. Because of an unusual event that took place just before her death, Clare has been declared the patron saint of television. Legend has it that she could not attend Mass, so the holy ceremony appeared miraculously on the convent wall.

Francis of Assisi was still filled with the tales and legends of the past, and when the Crusades were reported to him, he decided to visit the Holy Land himself. The "Holy Land" is the name given to the region in which Jesus Christ was born and raised. Many sites in that area are considered sacred because our Lord visited them and spoke to the people there. The Crusades were being conducted in order to free the cities from Muslim rulers, who had conquered them over the years.

After a disastrous attempt to make his pilgrimage to the Holy Land in 1212, during which time Francis was shipwrecked and ill, he started again in 1214 but was unable to travel on. Finally, in 1219, still filled with the legends of honor and valor, of knights and sacred oaths, Francis and his companion, Brother Illuminato, arrived at Damietta, in modern Egypt. There he saw six thousand Crusaders die in a battle, and he was filled with horror at the loss of human life. The Crusaders were also going against their vows as knights and as Christians, becoming cruel and brawling in the streets. Shamed by the sight of them, Francis started out into the desert, looking for the camp of the sultan Malik al-Kamil, who was the nephew of the famed Islamic warrior Saladin.

It was a dangerous trek, because the Muslims kept watch on their lands, and he and Brother Illuminato could have been killed. They were caught by one patrol, actually, and they kept shouting for the "sultan" so that the soldiers would deliver them alive to Malik al-Kamil's tent. When he did arrive in the sultan's presence, Francis was shocked and intrigued.

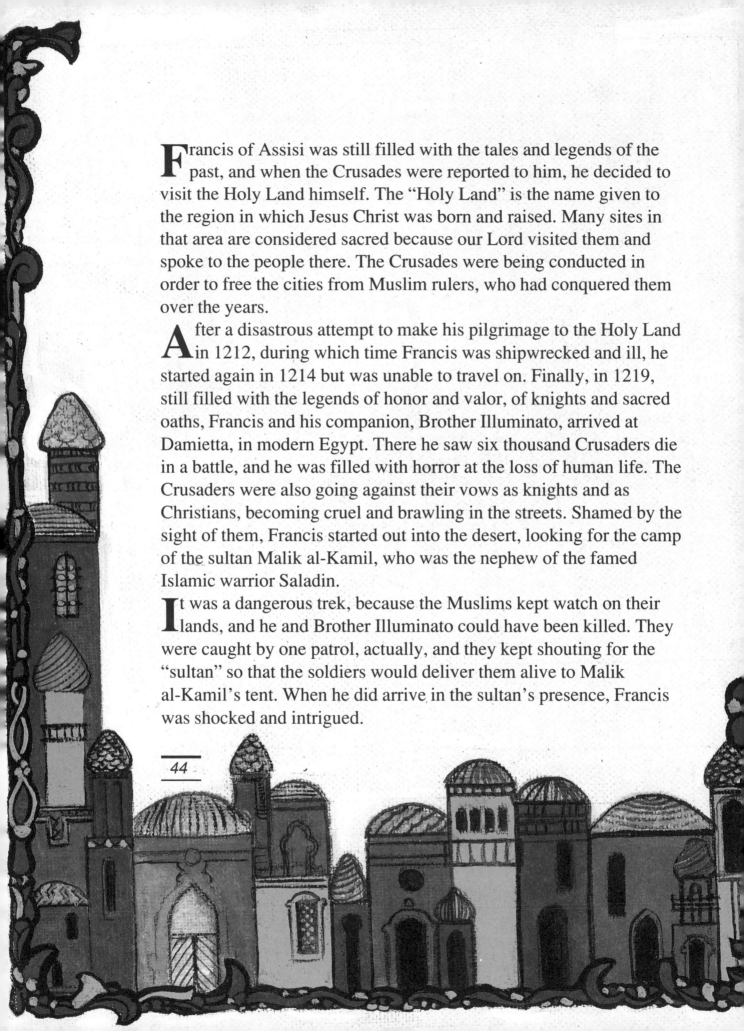

Dragged before the Islamic ruler, Francis discovered a man who was highly intelligent, cultured, and wise in medicine and literature. It seems that Malik al-Kamil was one of the most educated people that Francis ever met. He had an interest in many subjects and was delighted to meet the two Franciscans.

Many legends have come down about Francis' meeting with the sultan, including one that claimed that he offered to walk through fire in order to convert his Muslim host. Malik al-Kamil told Francis through an interpreter that the Christianity which he described was very beautiful. He also said that it was impossible for him to accept Christ, as it was impossible for Francis to deny Him. Malik al-Kamil added that if either one converted he would be dead by morning. It was enough that two men had met in peace, had talked about faith and love.

The sultan offered many gifts to Francis as he set him free, all of which Francis declined courteously. Then he gave the Franciscans the kindest present of all. Francis and Illuminato were to have safe passage through all of the holy places of the region. The two men were escorted out of the desert and shown the way to Acre, where the Crusaders had a magnificent fortress. Acre was one of the last strongholds to fall to Islam and was the home base of the great Crusader knight orders.

The sultan's safe-conduct was respected by all of the Muslim forces in the region. Malik al-Kamil was the nephew of Saladin and a powerful man who could reach out his arm to crush anyone disobedient to his will. Francis had faced the ordeal and had won the respect of the ruler.

If all this journeying seems strange, it must be remembered that during the Middle Ages men and women went on pilgrimages, particularly to the places where Christ had lived. Francis of Assisi, once the spoiled darling, came out of the desert a true warrior. He was a ragged little man in brown, called the "Poverello," or the little poor man, and he still laughed and sang songs to God. Underneath, however, was a will of iron.

He was free of ambitions, free of fear of what others might think or say, and free of the need to be popular. Because of this wholeness, this liberty, the sultan recognized him as a true holy man. Francis, who called himself "Brother Ass" because he knew that he was stubborn and proud, has always been honored in that part of the world. He looked like a beggar, but he had the heart of a lion. Nothing on earth could chain him or break his spirit. Like the eagles in the sky, Francis was flying straight into the sun.

Yet another ruler was about to discover the Poverello, as he was about to hear the questions that Francis asked of life. His name was John of Brienne, and he was the Christian king of Jerusalem. The king was actually a relative of Walter of Brienne, the man who had been Francis' ideal of chivalry and knightly honor decades before. John and Francis met while journeying to Syria, and John was changed as a result. After Francis' death he became a Friar Minor, which is the title used to describe Franciscans even to this day. John of Brienne asked to be buried in Assisi upon his death, which took place in 1237.

47

In July 1220, Brother Stephen arrived in Acre to tell Francis about troubles in the Franciscan Brotherhood. There were now Franciscans throughout most of Europe, as young men had come flocking to their houses. Some of the brighter Franciscans, in fact, had become bishops of the Church and had power and rank.

Of course, with so many men involved, there was no way that all of them could be trained to live the Rule as Francis desired. A few peculiar ones had been accepted as well in good faith. Some lived in stone houses, ate fancy meals, and wore fine clothes. Still others started Franciscan houses without bothering to tell anyone or to ask for permission. They all wanted to be like Francis of Assisi, but not all of them understood what his life embraced.

Francis returned to Italy immediately and went to see Cardinal Ugolino, who would become the future Pope Gregory IX. Cardinal Ugolino became the patron of the Brotherhood and directed the more than five thousand men who were following in Francis' footsteps toward perfection.

Francis also created a new and marvelous group of lay men and women, people in the world who wanted to live as Franciscans. This was called the Third Order of St. Francis, and today thousands of men and women serve Christ in the world with the ideals and love that Francis taught them.

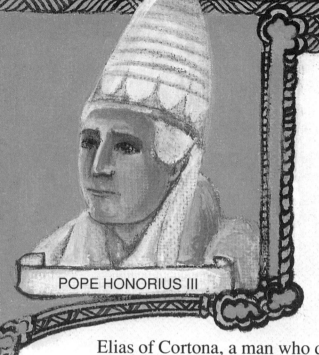

POPE HONORIUS III

On September 27, 1220, with the publishing of the papal document *Cum Secundum*, Pope Honorius III gave his blessing to the Franciscan Order. It was a truly historic occasion, and the Franciscans celebrated until they heard the news that Francis was retiring as the head of the Order.

Peter of Catania was chosen in his place, followed within the year by Elias of Cortona, a man who did not entirely approve of Francis' ideals. Francis went to Fonte Colombo, where he dictated the new Rule of the Order to Brother Leo. Others, hearing the new regulations, however, brought up the old arguments about Francis' way of life. They felt that he was too harsh, too austere — which means too hard on himself — and his spirit of absolute poverty would end up killing half the Franciscans. Some claimed that it was bad enough that Francis was killing himself with his fasts, his work, and his prayers. He could not be allowed to take five thousand more with him into an early grave.

Here one has to understand that many times the human beings who begin great adventures, particularly those of the spirit, see their original dreams fade in the changes that come with success. The austerity — the rules about sleeping on boards or on the ground, the simple meals, the heavy work — was practical only when a small group followed Francis. Large groups needed another kind of rule, another kind of discipline, especially if the Order was to grow and stay vital in changing times.

Francis made no complaints as the Rule was altered. He went to a small cave at Greccio, called a hermitage. There he prayed and watched, seeing his life turning into another type of adventure, one that would bring pain and suffering. Before he accepted that burden, however, Francis had another gift for the world. On Christmas, 1223, he presented everyone with a lasting present, one that people still enjoy today. Francis decided that people needed to see the stable at Bethlehem for themselves in order to understand the Savior's birth.

He arranged a manger, with hay and animals, with the sights and sounds of that first Nativity scene, and the people came to kneel before the Prince of Peace with new understanding and new hearts. Many marvelous things took place that day. The Christ Child appeared in Francis' arms, and when the people took the hay home to their sick animals, the animals were cured. In time the custom of having a Nativity scene spread elsewhere, and the French named the scene a *crèche*. Throughout the Christian world, to this day, people still wonder at the Prince of Peace in His manger on Christmas.

As the Order took on a new and lasting form, Francis stayed hidden in his hermitage. His life was changed. He had offered to imitate Christ, and God had taken him at his word. No one can presume to follow Christ without taking up the cross, and Francis faced suffering in his last days. Alone, seeing his original work altered by others, half blind because of his time in the desert of Malik al-Kamil, Francis was failing. He would soon vanish from the earth, forgotten, just a memory or a legend. Almighty God, however, once again entered Francis' life in a vivid — a bright and dramatic — sense. The ragged little man in brown was to bear the symbols of his dedication for the world to see.

On a mountain called La Verna, Francis, along with Brothers Leo, Rufino, and Angelo, was praying and suffering. His sight was dimmed because of the sun in the desert and because of the treatments that the local doctors had prescribed. He was exhausted and alone in spirit, cut loose from the Brotherhood, which had become an Order.

On September 14, 1224, Leo found Francis in the nearby wooded area, surrounded by a light. Francis was being visited by a six-winged seraphim, one of the great angelic choirs, but within the wings was a man nailed to a cross. Staring at the vision, Francis felt blood dripping from his own hands and feet, and from his side, as he received the stigmata, the sign of the cross embedded on human flesh.

51

His companions, stunned by what had happened, helped Francis keep the news of his stigmata hidden for as long as possible. He did not want people coming out of curiosity or out of concern, preferring to remain in peace and in prayer for as long as possible. In time, naturally, a word was dropped here and there as others saw telltale signs. Before long the story raced like a fire throughout the region, and the people began to flock to Francis' retreat.

He was nearing the end of his time on earth, partly because of the way he had treated his own body, Brother Ass. His stomach, liver, and diaphragm were in a state of collapse. Elias of Cortona, who had become the head of the Order, had a vision of Francis' coming death. That news upset Elias, but Francis welcomed it.

After a small tour of the area, Francis reached San Damiano, and his companions had to keep people from tearing off his robe for souvenirs. In Rieti, meanwhile, the Pope had established a temporary residence because of riots in Rome. Francis was brought there, but it did him little good. All kinds of famous people interrupted his prayers and his rest, and the leaders of his world pushed their way into his recovery room.

Elias finally arranged for Francis to go to Bagnara, which was a spa area, with cool, clean air and fresh water. Francis' condition worsened, however, setting many people into a state of panic. It was feared that people from other towns would kidnap Francis just to have the privilege of saying that he died in their city. Assisi's leaders sent a band of mounted knights to escort Francis back to the Portiuncula, and they proved tender companions, carrying him in their arms.

After several delays, Francis was returned to his beloved Portiuncula. There he asked to be placed on the ground, where he could pray and sing with the Brothers as they recited the *Canticle of the Sun*, a hymn that he had composed. All around him his Brothers and admirers were weeping, but Francis accepted the coming of Sister Death, as he called this terrible mystery that faces all human beings. He told everyone that "death, which is the gateway of life, is at hand." Smiling, assuring them all of his joy and his expectations, Francis died peacefully.

Many claimed that they saw his soul arise in a shower of light. Some distance away, at Terra di Lavoro, a Brother Augustine, who had been ill for some time, sat up in his bed and cried out: "Wait for me, Father, wait for me! Behold, I am coming with you!" When his companions asked who he was talking about, Augustine announced: "Do you not see our father Francis going to heaven?" Brother Augustine smiled knowingly and died.

Francis of Assisi appeared to many after his death, and through his intercessions — his pleas on behalf of his fellow human beings — many miracles took place. Assisi became the center of new spirituality, as pilgrims arrived to honor the Poverello personally.

In 1228, just two years after his death, Francis was declared a saint by the Church, canonized in Rome. He has remained one of the most popular saints in the world, shining as a mirror of Christ, reminding everyone of the beauty of God's world and the joys of learning to live in imitation of Christ while on earth.

ST. FRANCIS OF ASSISI

The Prayer of St. Francis

Lord, make me an instrument of Your peace.
Where there is hatred, let me sow love;
Where there is injury, pardon;
Where there is discord, unity;
Where there is doubt, faith;
Where there is despair, hope;
Where there is darkness, light;
Where there is sadness, joy.
Lord, grant that I may seek rather to comfort than to be
comforted,
To understand rather than to be understood,
To love rather than to be loved.
For it is in giving that one receives,
It is in forgiving that one is forgiven,
And it is in dying that one awakens to eternal life.

56